Five Paper Ducks

by

Carly Easton

photography by

John Lei

Macmillan McGraw-Hill

New York   Farmington

Cut, cut, cut.

Just like so.

Five paper ducks

in a row.

Cut, cut, cut.

A little more.

A mother duck

and her baby ducks four.

Cut, cut, cut.

What is it then?

But you can just start again.